BLockhead

THE LiFe OF FiBONacci

Joseph D'Agnese

Illustrated by John O'Brien

Henry Holt and Company · New York

For easier reading, we have changed the place names of certain countries to their modern names. We have altered Hindu-Arabic numerals to appear the way they do today as well. They would have looked slightly different in Fibonacci's day.

Henry Holt and Company
Publishers since 1866
120 Broadway,
New York, NY 10271
mackids.com

Henry Holt® is a registered trademark of Henry Holt and Company, LLC.
Text copyright © 2010 by Joseph D'Agnese
Illustrations copyright © 2010 by John O'Brien
All rights reserved.

Library of Congress Cataloging-in-Publication Data
D'Agnese, Joseph.
Blockhead: the story of Fibonacci / Joseph D'Agnese ;
illustrated by John O'Brien. — 1st ed.
p.   cm.
ISBN 978-0-8050-6305-9
1. Fibonacci, Leonardo, ca. 1170–ca. 1240—Juvenile literature.
2. Mathematicians—Italy—Biography—Juvenile literature.
3. Fibonacci numbers—Juvenile literature. I. O'Brien, John, ill. II. Title.
QA29.F5D34 2010   510.92—dc22   [B]   2009005264

First Edition—2010 / Designed by Véronique Lefèvre Sweet
Printed in China by RR Donnelley Asia Printing Solutions Ltd., Dongguan City,
Guangdong Province

20   19   18   17   16   15   14

For my parents,
Frank and Angela
—J. D.

You can call me Blockhead.
Everyone else does.

One day when I was just a boy, Maestro wrote out a
math problem and gave us ten minutes to solve it.
    I solved it in two seconds.

That's the way I am with numbers. I have loved them since I was very little. Everywhere I looked in my parents' home, there was something to count.

That day in class, the other students did their math
on abacuses and wrote out their answers in Roman
numerals. It was time-consuming, but that's how we
did our math back then.

As I waited for them to finish, I got bored.

I counted twelve birds in a tree outside. How many legs did all those birds have? I wondered. How many eyes? How many wings? And if each bird sang for two seconds, one bird after the other, how long would it take all of them to sing?

These were such beautiful questions that I started daydreaming.

9

"Leonardo!" cried Maestro. "How dare you daydream in my class!"

"But, sir," I said, "I was thinking—"

"A-ha!" Maestro cried. "There's the trouble! There will be no thinking in this classroom—only working! You're nothing but an absent-minded, lazy dreamer, you . . . you

BLOCKHEAD!"

The other kids laughed.

"BLOCKHEAD! BLOCKHEAD!" they cried.

I was so sad that I ran out of school and into the streets of Pisa.

I let the noise of the city swallow me up. What a wonderful city it was! The year was 1178, and Pisa was one of the greatest cities in all of Italy.

13

In the churchyard, workers were building a new bell tower. Something had gone seriously wrong with the builder's math!

All around me I saw and heard the glory of numbers. So many people were using math in their work. My head was swimming.

14

I was so excited that I didn't watch where
I was going. "Stop dreaming!" a lady cried.
"What are you, a blockhead?"

That night, my father was angry. "The whole city is talking!" he yelled. "Everyone says my son is an idiot. They call you Blockhead. I can't have that."

"Perhaps you are being too hard on the boy, Signor Bonaccio," said my father's adviser, Alfredo.

"Silence!" cried father. "Leonardo, soon you will leave with me for Africa. That will put an end to these nicknames. I'll make a merchant of you yet!"

"Yuck," I thought. "Who wants to be a merchant?"

The night before we sailed, I couldn't sleep. I watched sadly as a shooting star fell into the ocean.

In the star's light I saw an old friend. He waited for me to dry my tears.

"I think people are happiest when they know what pleases them," said Alfredo. "Me, I love cheese. And you, Master Leonardo, what makes you happiest?"

"Numbers," I said without thinking.

"Then you should learn all you can about them. That way you will always be happy."

I decided to take Alfredo's advice. My father took me to live in a city called Bugia in northern Africa. In my new home, I noticed that the Arab merchants didn't use Roman numerals. They used numerals they had borrowed from the Hindu people of India.

Back home, we wrote this: XVIII.

Here, the merchants wrote this: 18.

See how much easier it is?

I wanted so much to learn these numerals.

By day I did my father's accounts. At night Alfredo went with me as I learned the strange new numerals.

When I got older, my father sometimes sent me on business trips. When I wasn't working, I sought out wise men in every city.

In Egypt, I learned how the ancient pharaohs and their subjects had used fractions.

I measured my way through Istanbul, Turkey, and Damascus, Syria.

In Greece, I learned about geometry from ancient books of math.

In Sicily, I put my division and subtraction skills to good use.

In France . . . well . . . in France I ate fish soup.

N
W · E
S

BLACK SEA
GREECE
MEDITERRANEAN SEA
SYRIA
EGYPT
RED SEA
23

One day I began to write a book about Hindu-Arabic numerals. I tossed some riddles into it, like this one:

There was a man who put two baby rabbits in a field. It takes rabbits one month to grow up and be ready to have babies. And it takes them one more month to give birth to a pair of baby rabbits.

Every month a pair of grown-up rabbits gives birth to
a new pair of baby rabbits.

How many pairs of rabbits will the man have at the
end of a year?

Alfredo tried to solve it, but he couldn't.

Then I showed him how to solve the problem.

On the very first day, you'd have 1 pair of baby rabbits.

At the end of Month 1, you'd have 1 pair all grown up and ready to have babies.

End of Month 2: 1 grown-up pair, 1 baby pair.

End of Month 3: 2 grown-up pairs, 1 baby pair.

End of Month 4: 3 grown-up pairs, 2 baby pairs.

End of Month 5: 5 grown-up pairs, 3 baby pairs. . . .

Then I noticed that you don't even have to write out the whole problem.

If you add any two consecutive numbers in the pattern, you'd get the next number:

1 pair + 1 pair = 2 pairs,

1 pair + 2 pairs = 3 pairs,

2 pairs + 3 pairs = 5 pairs.

Here are the first few numbers of the pattern: 1, 1, 2, 3, 5, 8, 13, 21, 34, 55, 89, 144, 233, 377.

If you don't watch out, you'll have 233 pairs of rabbits in a year! (Or 377 if you started with a grown-up pair.)

News of my work reached Frederick II, ruler of the Holy Roman Empire. When I visited his palace, his wise men challenged me with a bunch of really hard math problems. But I solved them in no time.

"This Leonardo is one smart cookie," said Frederick. Everyone laughed. After all, he was the emperor.

29

I felt proud of my accomplishments. But one day, when
I was back in Pisa, I overheard some people talking in the
marketplace.

"That's the son of Bonaccio," said a man. "He's the one
who says we should use those numerals from India."

"What's wrong with the old numerals?" asked another.
"If they were good enough for the Romans, they're good
enough for me!"

"What a blockhead!"

Suddenly I was sad again. "What good is all my work if people don't listen?" I thought. "People will always remember me as a blockhead."

I wondered what my old friend Alfredo would have said. Suddenly, it was as if he were there with me.

"Don't listen to these fools, Leonardo!" roared Alfredo. "Aren't these numbers of yours very important?"

"I certainly think so!" I said. "Someday Hindu-Arabic numerals will be known all over the world. Why, the more I study them, the more amazed I am by them!"

With that, I pointed to a flower on the beach. "How many petals does this flower have?"

Alfredo counted and answered, "Twenty-one."

"And this flower?"

"Thirteen," he replied. "So what?"

But I did not reply quickly. Instead, we walked along the beach all night, counting things.

We counted three-petal flowers, five-petal flowers, and eight-petal flowers. We counted to five on the arms of a starfish and inside an apple.

"See, Alfredo?" I said. "In everything that I count, everywhere that I look, I keep finding the same numbers. Do you recognize them?"

Alfredo recited them aloud. "1, 1, 2, 3, 5, 8, 13, 21, 34, 55 . . . my goodness," he cried. "They are the numbers from your rabbit problem!"

"Exactly," I said. "And we're just getting started!"

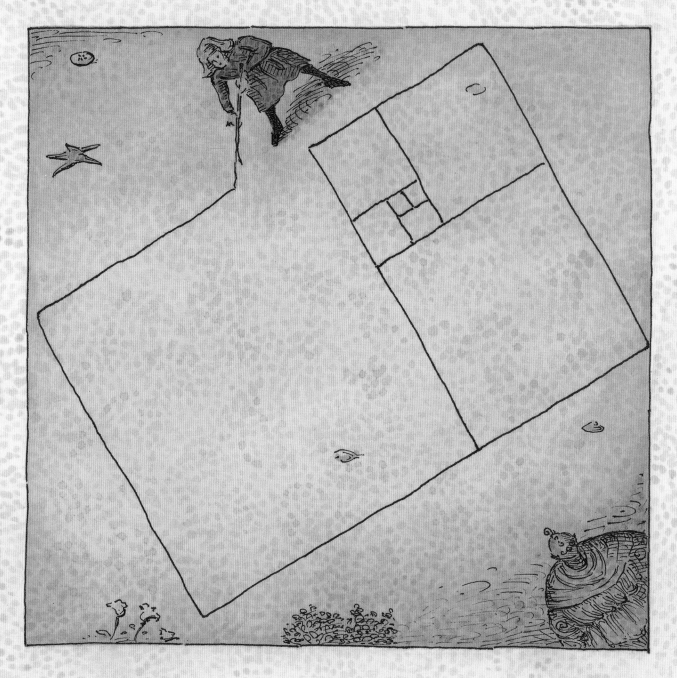

"Lately I've been thinking about those numbers in a *different* way. Watch!"

In the sand I drew one tiny square and one more tiny square next to it.

Next came a shape two squares high and two squares wide. Then a three-by-three square shape.

Then a five-by-five square shape, an eight-by-eight square shape, and a thirteen-by-thirteen square shape.

"I could go on and on," I said, "but it just wouldn't look right unless I connected them . . . like this."

Can you guess what I drew inside them? Alfredo sure couldn't.

"A spiral!" I shouted. "You can make a spiral with my numbers!"

"How magnificent!" said Alfredo.

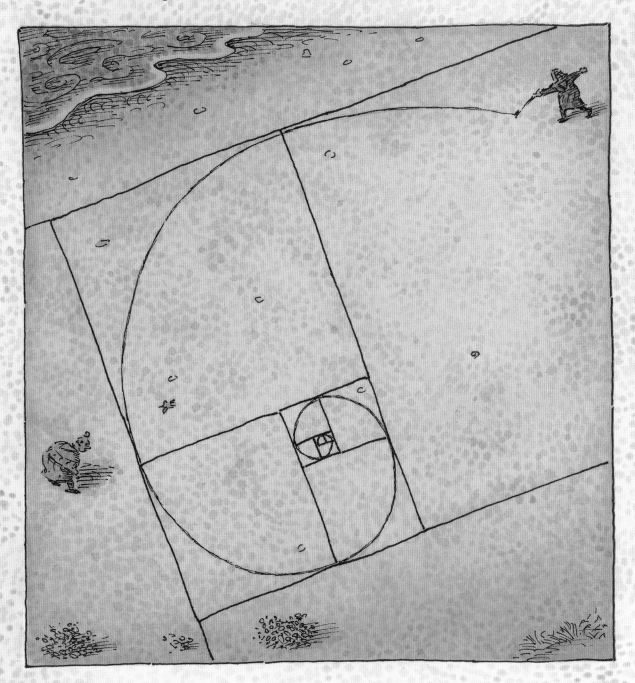

"Yes, it is," I said. "But I still don't understand *why* these numbers are so special."

"Don't you see, Leonardo?" said Alfredo. "These are the numbers Mother Nature uses to order the universe. She has hidden them in many places. And until now, no one has found her secret."

Alfredo's words filled my heart with joy. All my life people had called me Blockhead because I daydreamed about numbers. But how could that be bad? Mother Nature loved numbers too!

Alfredo was delighted. "From the tiniest plant to the prettiest pinecone, from the tallest flower to the wettest wave to the most wondrous, far-off galaxy . . . all these are home to your numbers, Leonardo."

I am old now, but numbers still make me happy. In all my years, I have never told anyone the secret I shared with Alfredo that night.

But now I've told you.

Look through this book again and you will find my numbers just as they are in real life. Now you see why I don't mind being called Blockhead, after all!

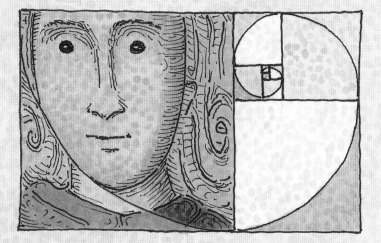

Leonardo of Pisa

(1170?–1240?)

Little is known about the life of the mathematician called Leonardo Fibonacci. This story is based on the few things we do know—and a bit of make-believe. His nickname, Bigollo, can be translated as "wanderer" or "traveler." It may also mean "idler, dreamer, or lazy person." In other words, a blockhead.

Today, Leonardo is considered the greatest Western mathematician of the Middle Ages. A statue of him stands in Pisa, Italy, not far from the famous Leaning Tower. And the Hindu-Arabic numerals that he worked so hard to introduce to the world are the very same ones we use today.

For all his work, Leonardo is best known for the number pattern that appeared in his famous rabbit problem, a pattern we call the Fibonacci Sequence. (Fibonacci means "son of Bonaccio.") Scientists and mathematicians now know that the sequence is special: It's a blueprint that describes how living things such as flowers grow in an orderly, harmonious way. The numbers even pop up in works of human imagination—buildings, music, art, and poetry.

And yet, say historians, Leonardo never realized the importance of these numbers.

Or did he?